PEOPLE WHO HELP US

Popcorn

Ambulance Crew

Honor Head

D1323885

Explore the world with **Popcorn** - your complete first non-fiction library.

Look out for more titles in the Popcorn range. All books have the same format of simple text and striking images. Text is carefully matched to the pictures to help readers to identify and understand key vocabulary. www.waylandbooks.co.uk/popcorn

Published in paperback in 2013 by Wayland
Copyright © Wayland 2013

Wayland
Hachette Children's Books
338 Euston Road
London NW1 3BH

Wayland Australia
Level 17/207 Kent Street
Sydney NSW 2000

Produced for Wayland by
White-Thomson Publishing Ltd
www.wtpub.co.uk
+44 (0)843 208 7460

Editor: Jean Coppendale
Designer: Clare Nicholas
Picture Researcher: Amy Sparks
Series consultant: Kate Ruttle
Design concept: Paul Cherrill

Produced with the assistance of South Western
  Ambulance Service NHS Trust

Head, Honor.
  Ambulance crew. -- (Popcorn. People who help us)
  1. Ambulance service--Pictorial works--Juvenile
  literature.
  I. Title II. Series
  362.1'88-dc22

ISBN: 978 0 7502 7206 3

Wayland is a division of Hachette Children's Books,
an Hachette UK company.
www.hachette.co.uk

Printed and bound in China

Photographs:
Alamy: Gregory Wrona 1/12/23bl, Roy Childs 20;
Dreamstime: Andres Rodriguez 4; Franklin Watts:
Chris Fairclough 7, 11/22; Photolibrary: 5/23tl; St John
Ambulance; 20; Wayland: Chris Fairclough 6/cover, 9,
10/23tr, 13, 14/23br, 15, 16, 17/2, 18, 19

⊕ Contents

# Ambulance

We call an ambulance when there is an emergency. An emergency is when there is an accident or someone suddenly becomes sick.

The ambulance takes people who are very ill to hospital.

4

If there is a road accident or a fire,
an ambulance will come to help
anyone who is hurt.

The ambulance crew will take an injured person to hospital.

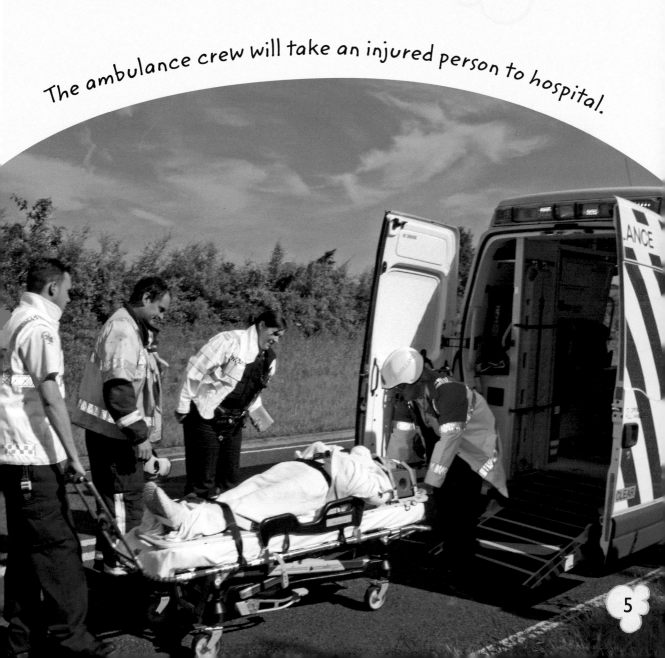

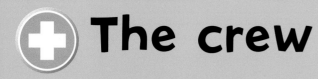 The crew

There are usually two people called the crew in each ambulance. One person is a paramedic and the other is a technician.

The paramedic and technician work together as a team.

The ambulance crew has lots of training so they can look after sick and injured people. They use plastic models for training.

Paramedics and technicians are not doctors but they can give people medicine.

This technician is using a model to learn how to start someone's breathing after an accident.

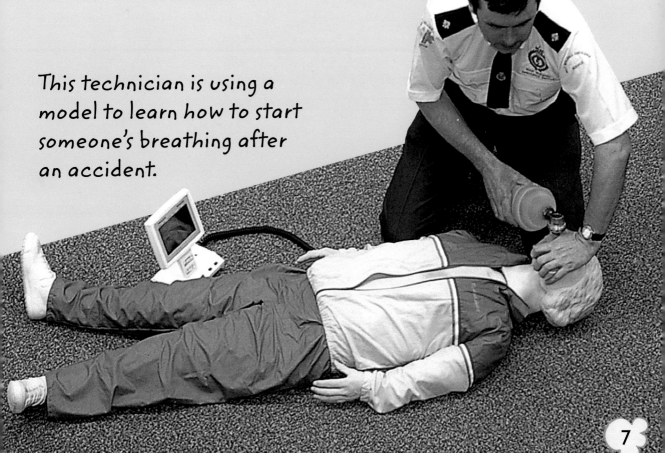

⊕ Emergency!

The ambulance crew work from an ambulance station. This is where the ambulances are kept.

When there is an emergency the crew and ambulance are ready to go.

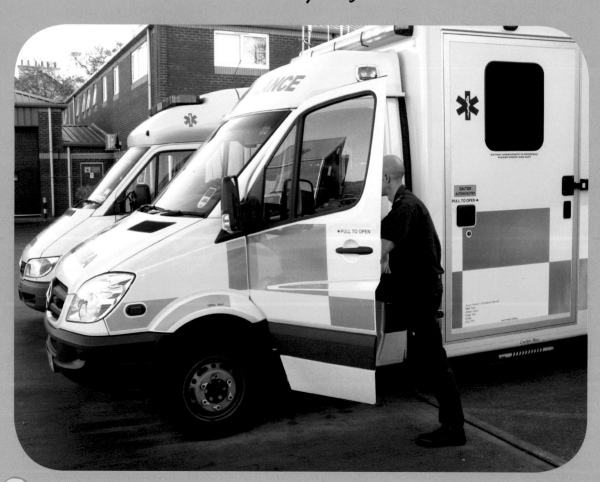

The ambulance has a siren that makes a loud noise. Other drivers on the road know that they must let the ambulance go first.

The ambulance crew is trained to drive an ambulance fast through busy streets.

The ambulance must get to the accident as quickly as possible.

 Ambulance equipment

Inside the ambulance there is a lot of equipment. This helps the crew to look after injured people.

While they are waiting for a call, the crew check all the equipment.

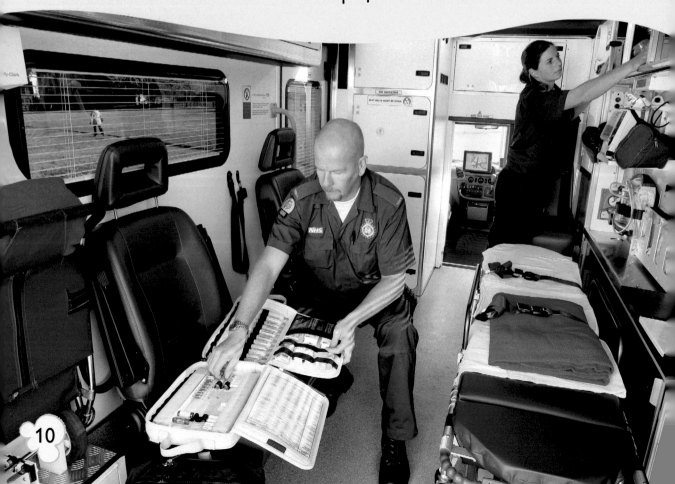

Some ambulances have a ramp so
the crew can push a wheelchair in
and out of the ambulance.

This lady needs an ambulance to take her
to the hospital because she is in a wheelchair.

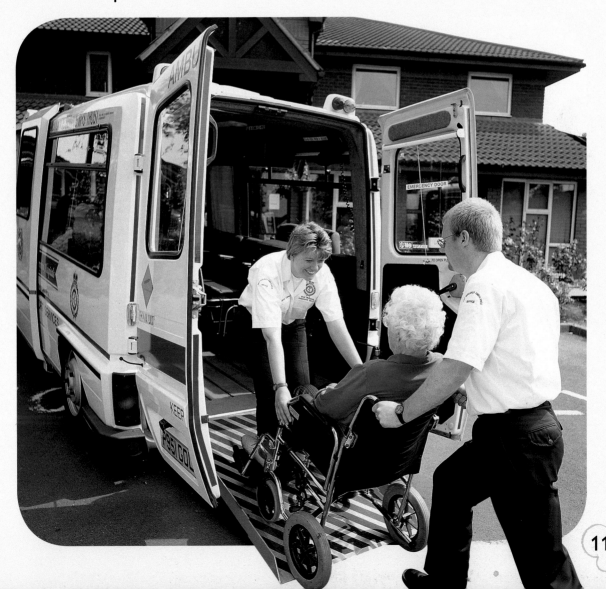

A road accident

At a road accident, the crew check anyone who is injured. They try to make them as comfortable as possible.

The paramedic's bag is full of medicines and first-aid equipment.

bag

The crew gently places the injured person on a stretcher. Then the person is put on a bed in the ambulance.

A moving platform lifts the stretcher in and out of the ambulance.

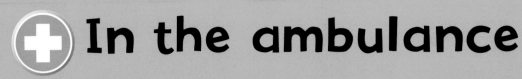 In the ambulance

On the way to the hospital, the paramedic gives the patient an oxygen mask to help her breathe.

A member of the crew stays with the patient in case she needs help on the way to the hospital.

oxygen mask

The ambulance takes the patient to the Accident and Emergency department at the hospital.

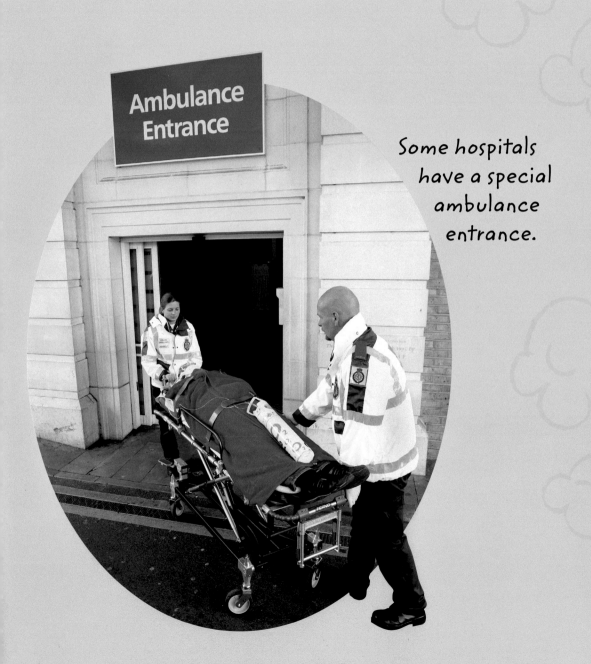

Some hospitals have a special ambulance entrance.

Ambulance Entrance

First responders

Paramedics with bikes and cars are part of the ambulance service. These are called first responders because they can get to an accident first.

Ambulance cars have lots of medicine and equipment in the back.

The driver of an ambulance bike wears a bright yellow jacket. The bike is also yellow so it can be seen in daylight or at night.

A motorbike can get through heavy traffic faster than an ambulance.

A first responder can save lives by getting to an emergency very quickly.

Calling an ambulance

To call an ambulance, dial 999.
Tell the operator answering the
phone you want an ambulance.

Give the operator your name and telephone number and the address where the ambulance is needed.

As soon as a call is made, the operator will pass the information to the nearest ambulance.

The crew can see where the emergency is on a special screen inside the ambulance.

Never dial 999 unless there is a real accident or emergency.

St John Ambulance

The St John Ambulance Brigade is an ambulance service run by volunteers who offer to do the work for free.

The crew help people at public events, such as music festivals and carnivals.

St John Ambulance also has a
first-aid group for young people.
The group is called Badgers.

These Badgers are learning how to look
after someone who has had an accident.

How does an ambulance crew help us?

Can you remember some of the jobs an ambulance crew does to help us?

Match the jobs below with the pictures.

1. Takes injured people to hospital.

2. Helps to look after injured people at an accident.

3. Looks after the injured person in the ambulance.

4. Checks all the equipment in the ambulance.

5. Takes people to hospital if they are in wheelchairs.

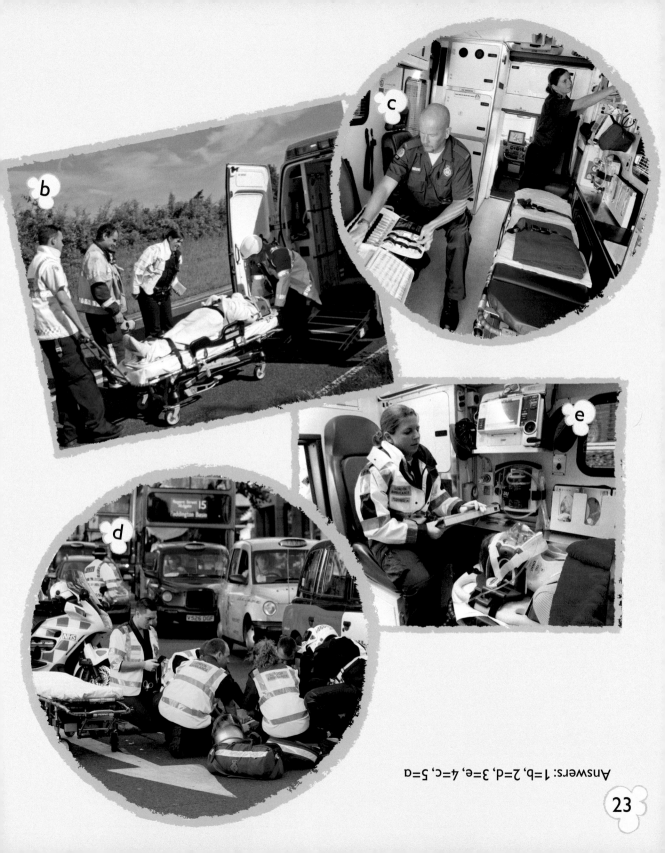

Glossary

oxygen air that helps us to breathe

paramedic ambulance worker trained to give people medicine and first aid

patient someone who is not well or who is injured

siren something that makes a loud noise on an ambulance so other cars will let them go by

technician ambulance worker who can give first aid

volunteer someone who helps for no payment

Index